Essays on The Banking Industry:
Solutions for Facilitating Optimized Capital Flows, Equitable Economic Growth, and Crises Resolution

Essays on The Banking Industry

Essays on The Banking Industry:
Solutions for Facilitating Optimized Capital Flows, Equitable Economic Growth, and Crises Resolution
ISBN: 9781729477458

© 2018 Hendrith Vanlon Smith Jr
© 2018 Mayflower-Plymouth Capital LLC
All Rights Reserved by way of the United States Copyright Office.

First Edition, Published 2016
This Edition, 2018.

Printed in The United States of America
IP Made in The USA

Essays on The Banking Industry

Essays on The Banking Industry:
Solutions for Facilitating Optimized Capital Flows, Equitable Economic Growth, and Crises Resolution

Contents

Introduction — 5

PART ONE: Applying the Principles of Permaculture-Capitalism™ to The Banking Industry — 7

PART TWO: FACILITATING OPTIMIZED CAPITAL FLOWS — 12

    Increasing Accessibility while retaining strong qualifications — 13

    Streamlining and Updating the Lending Process — 14

PART THREE: FACILITATING EQUITABLE ECONOMIC GROWTH — 15

    Investment as An Engine of Equity (from previous edition of Essays on The Banking Industry) — 17

    Reimagining the Role of the Branch Bank — 20

    Regulatory Prescriptions: CRA, etc. — 22

PART FOUR: FACILITATING CRISES RESOLUTION — 23

    Root Causes of Crises — 24

    Liquidity Management — 25

    Internal Risk Management — 26

    External Risk Management — 26

Works Cited — 27

Author Bio — 28

Essays on The Banking Industry

Introduction

The book is written from the perspective of a Central Banker for an audience of Retail Bankers and top leaders in the Banking/Financial Services Industry. It presents, essentially, prescriptions that may be applied by Retail Bankers (Executives of Banks) in order to (a) facilitate optimized capital flows in the economy, (b) facilitate equitable economic growth in the economy, and (c) help resolve systematic and broad societal crises when they arise - these all being ways that Banks may add value to customers in a way that is mutually beneficial and mutually profitable. In a sense, it is also a prescription for how to thrive in and add value in the Permaculture Economy (Permaculture-Capitalism). The book is intended to present a few simple ideas, simply - and not to be an exhaustive data intensive presentation. I have found that my strength as an author and speaker is in using data and analysis to simplify the complex, not the production of analysis itself.

The traditional view is that through the process of receiving deposits, initiating loans, and responding to interest rate signals from the Fed, the banking system helps to basically channel funds from savers to borrowers in an efficient manner. While this is true, it is not the whole truth. It is time for us to be more honest and more holistic in our acknowledgement of the role the banking industry plays in our Capitalist economy.

Now that we have set the objective, let's define the terms laid out in the title of this book: Capital Flows, Equitable Economic Growth, and Crises Resolution.

Capital [resource] flows refer to the movement of money for the purpose of investment, trade or business production, including the flow of capital [resources] within corporations in the form of investment capital, capital spending on operations and research and development (R&D). (Investopedia, 2018)

Equitable economic growth is about fostering a win-win economy. It includes harnessing the full potential of local economies by expanding opportunities and increasing the capacity for individuals and businesses to add value and obtain value (exchange value). The result is a stronger, more competitive economy where more people are prospering in their own way.

Crisis Resolution is about creating order out of chaos, solving societal problems, restoring normalcy and extracting value out of challenges. Our economy occasionally goes through crises, and the banking industry usually has a critical role in both causing and resolving the crisis.

In my experience and based on my assessment, these are the three core functions of the Banking Industry as a whole and of each individual participant in the industry. Thus, it calls upon our wisdom to address them and consider ways in which all industry participants may better execute these functions.

Essays on The Banking Industry

PART ONE:
Applying the Principles of Permaculture-Capitalism™ to The Banking Industry

The perspective of Permaculture Capitalism will allow Central Bankers to better execute the dual mandate and the five duties discussed above by (a) providing frameworks for more holistic assessment, and (b) providing frameworks for more holistic applications. It will allow Retail Bankers to better facilitate optimized capital flows, equitable economic growth and crises resolution.

Capitalism is an economic and political system in which a country's trade and industry are controlled by private owners for profit, rather than by the state/government (Google Dictionary, 2018). In the previous edition of Essays on Capitalism & The U.S. Economy, I spoke about "The Altruism of Capitalism" - my poetic way of describing how Capitalism, as defined here, is naturally good. "Capitalism is altruistic," I said, "...and it requires a certain altruism of each of us." I stand by these words and the theme persists in my work. Capitalism is good, however, it's not perfect. It is a tool - and as with any tool it can be misused, abused, misunderstood, and misapplied by ignorant and malicious people. Thats where permaculture comes in. Permaculture Capitalism is essentially the science of using the tool of Capitalism in perhaps a more altruistic way; toward greater scenarios of win-win and mutual prosperity for We The People. Regarding the Fed and the Central Bankers who execute its work, it will allow for greater execution of that work. Regarding the average citizen, it will foster an economy of greater prosperity and opportunity for advancement. Permaculture Capitalism is about sustainable, reciprocal, and mutual prosperity based on the efficient exchange of value."

Permaculture has its origins in farming. In the 20th Century, as farms became more monoculture (single-crop production), that led to higher yields in the short-term but an array of otherwise non-existent problems began to arise including soil erosion, increased pest populations, less nutritious/lower quality food, etc. That then prompted self-destructive reactions including the use of chemical pesticides and herbicides which also killed beneficial microbes, mycelium mycorrhiza, and pollinating bees, then the application of artificial fertilizer that cost more to produce than the value it added, etc. So monoculture farming morphed into a vicious cycle of impoverishment, inefficiency, boom-and-bust cycles (bull and bear markets), and costs that increasingly outweigh benefits. It's a very destructive and unsustainable model - wholly unable to be sustained - and kin to the most primitive kind of ignorance.

In a way, our economy today is also a monoculture of single-crop production, or at least shares the same primitive ignorance and the same lack of whole systems thinking as the monoculture farms of the 20th century. Permaculture Capitalism is a better approach to economics; more practical, more profitable, more wise.

Permaculture was a response to this destructive monoculture style of farming - a proposed solution. The word permaculture comes from two words meshed together - Permanent + Agriculture. The permaculture design principles focus on interconnectivity, diversity, and strengths complimenting to produce greater yields in a more efficient way and to the benefit of all participants. They are principles that may be, much to our satisfaction, applied to the organizing of our economy.

If we apply these Permaculture principles to Capitalism, we end up with an enhanced version of Capitalism - one that focuses more on the interconnectivity of economic actors (banks, businesses, consumers, schools, governments, municipalities, etc.), the efficient flow of resources through the economy, and greater yields (growth and profits) to the benefit of all participants. I call this Permaculture Capitalism.

For Reference, The Twelve Principles of Permaculture (in farming) Include:

1. Observe and interact. Permaculture relies on an understanding of specific site and local conditions.
2. Catch and store energy. ...
3. Obtain a yield. ...
4. Apply self-regulation and respond to feedback. ...

5. Use renewable resources. ...
6. Produce no waste. ...
7. Design from pattern to details. ...
8. Integrate rather than segregate.
9. Use Small and Slow Solutions – "Slow and steady wins the race" or "The bigger they are, the harder they fall" Small and slow systems are easier to maintain than big ones, making better use of local resources and produce more sustainable outcomes.
10. Use and Value Diversity – "Don't put all your eggs in one basket"
    Diversity reduces vulnerability to a variety of threats and takes advantage of the unique nature of the environment in which it resides.
11. Use Edges and Value the Marginal –
    The interface between things is where the most interesting things take place. These are often the most valuable, diverse and productive elements in the system.
12. Creatively Use and Respond to Change

Though these 12 principles were formulated for managing the natural ecosystem - with some imagination infused and a few substitutes of words, they may be creatively applied to the ecosystem that is our economy. And as these 12 principles bend nature toward our human desires of ecological productivity and natural yields, they may also bend our economy toward our human desires of economic productivity and commercial yields.

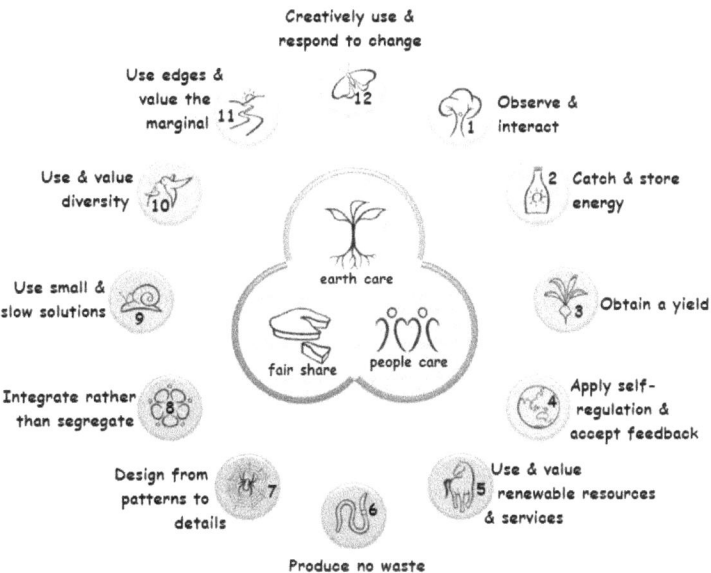

In a sense, each bank branch is a gardener of their local community, and may apply these 12 principles to the local capitalist economy.

PART TWO: FACILITATING OPTIMIZED CAPITAL FLOWS

Again, Capital flows refer to the movement of money and other resources through the economy for the purpose of investment, trade or business production. Each bank, and the banking industry as a whole, is a primary facilitator in this movement of money and other resources. They gather monetary resources from depositors, and allocate those resources to businesses and individuals looking to grow and expand. Through lending, banks also allow businesses of all kinds to engage in the production of new capital and other resources. A Bank lending to a Steel manufacturer, for example, facilitated (a) the flow of money/credit to the Steel manufacturer, (b) indirectly: the production of steel, and (c) indirectly: the production of human capital in the form of the skills required of the people whose labor (physical or mental) make the steel production possible, and (d) indirectly: the consumption of the steel by consumers - real estate developers, utensil makers, etc.

Essays on The Banking Industry

Increasing Accessibility while retaining strong qualifications

In many ways, access is an obscure barrier to capital for so many people. I'm not talking about subprime people, but just people on the margins - unskilled at technology perhaps, new to the english language, etc. It is not as if the banks do not want to work with these people, or that those people don't want to access capital - but the whole process is so complicated and convoluted that an obscure barrier prevents capital from flowing to and through these people.

From the perspective of access, startups like Robinhood, Stash, Acorns Investing, and comparatively new financial institutions like Quicken Loans are so good at facilitating access to capital flows for individuals that there is much to be learned by traditional banks that boast a 100 years of age as a baseline.

In my opinion, there will need to be vast improvements in the area of accessibility in order for the industry to reach full potential regarding the facilitation of optimized capital flows.

Streamlining and Updating the Lending Process

The lending process today is unnecessarily messy. Too many regulations dictate what banks can and cannot do, attempting to help borrowers but instead inhibiting borrowers and increasing overall default risk.

The lending process should be easy for borrowers in terms of knowing what is expected of them and being able to adhere to that expectation with clarity and simplicity. And as for the Banks, the process should be, with the exception of the necessary legal boundaries to protect all parties, free from restrictive and stifling regulation.

PART THREE: FACILITATING EQUITABLE ECONOMIC GROWTH

Again, equitable economic growth is about fostering a win-win economy, where all involved may prosper according to the value they provide. It includes harnessing the full potential of local economies and individuals by expanding opportunities and increasing the capacity for individuals and businesses to add value and obtain value (exchange value). The result is a stronger, more resilient, more competitive economy where more people are prospering in their own way.

One of the things that keep some groups of people from enjoying the benefits of economic growth is a barrier to entry into capital markets - that is, inability to borrow and invest. The ability to borrow and invest is largely tied to credit scores. I suggest we include all bill pay (non-debt) on credit reports moving forward, thus, in a sense, reducing the height of the lowest rung on the ladder so that those with less means (poor people) may be better able to get onto the ladder of economic opportunity and climb their way up.

Another thing we need to do is protect micro investing, otherwise known as fractional share investing. Fractional share investing allows poor people to begin investing without having to first acquire a large sum of capital or save for long period of time thus missing out on years of potential growth.

Entitlement reform/Welfare reform is another issue that must be addressed in this context. It is a strange irony, perhaps, but a truth nonetheless - that some of the very policies intended to help poor people infact do those same poor people incomprehensible harm. The amount of damage done in the name of goodness is shameful.

Educational system reform . We need to restore the value of the High School Diploma - a perfectly good measure of achievement that "progressives" have for some reason deemed worthless in todays market. It is not worthless, at least not inherently. Let's invest in our High Schools - include skills train in schools so that a diploma represents the acquisition of certain skills. Lets bring spirituality back into the schools so that we are developing the whole person toward knowledge, wisdom, and understanding. In order for growth to be equitable, we need people of various skillsets and levels of education to be able to participate, contribute to, and benefit from that growth. Banks have a role in this through partnerships and programs.

Investment as An Engine of Equity (from previous edition of Essays on The Banking Industry)

Banks should continue to facilitate investing for the average person. What exactly is an Investment? Both the informed and the uninformed may be surprised to know that it isn't as complicated as it seems. Essentially, an investment is a purchase of ownership in something that is expected to increase in value during the term of ownership. Whether the Currency is Time, Love or Money; and whether the Ownership is symbolized by a Bank account balance, a Stock Certificate, or something as intangible as Knowledge; we exchange the currency for an expected increase in value of the thing we own. We invest time in University expecting that the Degree earned will give us an increase of earning potential. We invest love in our family expecting that the love will increase our happiness and the happiness of our spouse and children. And we invest money into a business expecting that our partial ownership of that company will be worth more in the foreseeable future than it is at the time of initial investment. I care a lot about people, and I believe in "being my brothers keeper" and caring for those in need. And while I think some inequality is necessary and good, I believe poverty is not. I envision a world where we all are prospering and succeeding in life, though in different ways and to varying degrees. I would like to suggest a new way of promoting equity in our Capitalist society - investing in others, and empowering them to invest in themselves, in the marketplace, and in others. And

Essays on The Banking Industry

while donations and subsidies have their place, Investment may be a superior alternative. In our Capitalist-Democratic society, while levels of access may vary, access in and of itself is spread pretty evenly across all socioeconomic classes. A Millionaire certainly has greater access to ownership due to their higher purchasing power, but those of low income are just as able to invest as anyone else. A single share of General Motors currently sells for about $45.00 and as long as you have a record of being financially responsible with whatever money you have, you can open an investment account. And while a single share doesn't amount to wealth, it is a step on a long ladder to Equity. With persistence and sacrifice, a single share can become 10 shares; 10 shares can become 100 shares; 100 shares can become 1000 shares; and so on. We often think of Policy as the great engine of equity - "if only this Bill or this Law would pass." "If only that Legislation would be removed...." While Civic Engagement is Vital to the success of our Democracy, it may be time that we consider Investment the Great Equity Engine of our time - both investing in others and empowering them to invest. Maybe it's time we stop trying to give the poor temporary fixes to their poverty, and instead empower them with the tools they need to build themselves up as we have by investing in them and empowering them to invest. This would be a Win-Win scenario where both sides would see a good ROI given both sides are financially responsible and steward the investment wisely. Milton Friedman said it best, "There is no such thing as a free lunch." And giving people a free lunch in the name of equality or equity is counterproductive. Wouldn't it make more sense to invest in them - and to help them invest in themselves and in others - to help them build a kitchen and stock their pantry that they may

Essays on The Banking Industry

cook their own lunch instead of begging for it, and that they may then be to another as we were to them - an investor. Sometimes love, must be hard love. Hard things often take more time and effort to build, but provide more value.

Essays on The Banking Industry

Reimagining the Role of the Branch Bank

The evolving role of the branch bank will be an interesting thing to witness. Right now, scores of people are talking about how hundreds of branches are closing all across the nation because statistically people are going to the branch less often and they are using digital banking more frequently and more holistically. Those scores of people are right, and wrong. Digital banking will continue to play a pivotal role in retail banking. We will see greater technological advances that allow clients to manage their money online by themselves. But the need for a physical space dedicated to financial wellbeing is no more in threat of extinction than the need for a physical space to heal the sick. Advances in medicine have not eliminated the hospital, they have allowed for more creative ways to help people achieve health and avoid sickness. Advances in Digital banking will not eliminate the branch, the will allow for more creative ways to help people achieve financial well-being. Also consider this; just as the socio-political landscape is continually changing, the financial-economic landscape is also continually changing. Clients will always and forever-more need financial experts to help them navigate and effectively capitalize on the present financial-economic reality. Just as well as we will always need lawyers to help us navigate and capitalize on the present socio-political reality, and teachers to help us adapt to new demands on knowledge and skills. The transactional role of the bank is what will almost disappear. The bank will be a place for helping people achieve financial well-being - where clients and Financial Service Representatives have thorough conversations and Financial Service Representatives provide in-depth solutions to help people make, save and grow money. I see branches coming back full circle to a new place of significance in the life of the people in the community. Branch Financial Service Representatives will begin to take on more advisory roles with increased capacity to fulfill tasks that they once would have referred to a specialist on the insurance or investment teams, or to the back office. 10 years from now, when a client visits the branch, it will not be to conduct transactions as it was 10 years ago. Instead, they will visit the branch to sit with and receive financial consultation from a Financial Service Representatives - to help them structure their finances for tax efficiency, to help them capitalize on new financial sector laws and adapt to expired ones. Financial Service Representatives 10 years from now will be series 6 and 7 licensed, Insurance licensed, and more. They will be able to place trades for clients and give investment advice, manage portfolios, assist with insurance claims and more. The branch bank used to be one of the centers of American life. I'm bold enough to predict that it will be again in an even more intimate way.

Regulatory Prescriptions: CRA, etc.

The **Community Reinvestment Act** (CRA) is federal legislation enacted in 1977 with the intent of encouraging depository institutions to help meet the credit needs of surrounding **communities** (particularly low and moderate income neighborhoods). (Investopedia, 2018)

The CRA is perverse to say the least - a kind of economic affirmative action that does more harm than good. It's these kind of top down dictatorial policy prescriptions that, figuratively, kill the American soul. Instead of forcing banks to originate sub-prime loans, a better way is invest in the hearts and minds of low and moderate income people. A better way is to teach them how to be wise with money, how to save and invest, how to improve their credit score. That would be a win win. From the Banks perspective, each Bank must take some responsibility here too. If Banks would be more proactive about doing the right thing - regulators, policy makers, and activists would be less likely and have less ground to inact these kind of destructive policies.

Essays on The Banking Industry

PART FOUR: FACILITATING CRISES RESOLUTION

The ability for Banks to respond to both economic and social crises is of vital importance to the Fed, to Banks themselves, and to every citizen in the United States of America. It is in our collective best interest, if banks have sufficient liquidity to respond to runs, and to respond to the liquidity needs of customers responding to crises in their broader economy.

Root Causes of Crises

Economic crises is caused by one or more crises that occur within the economy, having large impact on other areas within the economy. It doesn't have to be related to stock prices or banks at all - it may be a drought on millions of acres of farmland, it may be a national security attack, or anything else. All thing affect and are affected by the economy.

A financial crisis occurs when institutions or assets are overvalued, and also by irrational investor behavior. A fast string of selloffs can then cause lower asset prices or more savings withdrawals. If no remedy is applied, this can cause an economy to go into a recession or depression.

Essays on The Banking Industry

Liquidity Management

Part of being prepared to resolve financial crises is determined by the management of liquidity. Part of this is determined by the reserve requirements set by The Federal Reserve Bank, which are currently as follow:

Reserve Requirements

Liability Type	Requirement	
	% of liabilities	Effective date
Net transaction accounts		
$0 to $16.3 million	0	1-17-19
More than $16.3 million to $124.2 million	3	1-17-19
More than $124.2 million	10	1-17-19
Nonpersonal time deposits	0	12-27-90
Eurocurrency liabilities	0	12-27-90

I believe 10% is too low of a reserve requirement to be sufficient, and I would be in favor of raising the reserve requirement to 16% for all banks regardless of size.

Each Bank is also responsible for Liquidity management beyond the scope of the reserve requirements, and should be expected to manage their portfolio in alignment with the values of Permaculture Capitalism.

Essays on The Banking Industry

Internal Risk Management

The 'Stress Test' put out by the Fed certainly helps with Internal Risk Management, but Banks really need to hold themselves more accountable to managing risk.

External Risk Management

Bank Holding Companies are financially involved in almost all big projects in the economy. So they can do much to manage risk in the broader economy including (a) prevention of default, (b) insuring against losses - in all cases, the bank and the community share mutual benefit in this extended risk management on the part of the bank.

Works Cited

1. https://www.thebanker.com/
2. www.nasw.org
3. https://www.thebalance.com/u-s-economic-crisis-3305668
4. https://en.wikipedia.org/wiki/Financial_crisis
5. www.investopedia.com
6. https://www.investopedia.com/articles/economics/09/financial-crisis-review.asp
7.

Author Bio

Hendrith Vanlon Smith Jr, born August 15 1989, is a Virginia Banker and Macro Social-Worker most known for his book 'The Wealth Reference Guide: An American Classic.' Hendrith earned his Bachelor of Science in Business Administration from Bethune-Cookman University (BCU), Studied Social Work at Howard University (HU), and earned his High School Diploma from Potomac High School in Maryland. He lives in Northern Virginia in the Washington DC metropolitan area. Hendrith has authored five books; The Wealth Reference Guide, Essays on Capitalism & The U.S. Economy, Essays on The Banking Industry, and The Pursuit of Happiness. He is the owner of Mayflower-Plymouth Capital LLC, a small real estate investment business based in Virginia.

Essays on The Banking Industry

Hendrith grew up in Southern Maryland, in a suberb of Washington DC named Prince Georges County. Both of his parents were lawyers who also attended BCU and HU.

http://g.co/kgs/stzu59
Google Knowledge Panel